From one alchemist
to another:

May we work our
own brand of magic
in Yemen, Timbuctoo,
or Kalamazoo.

W9-APK-301

Notes of an Alchemist

ALSO BY LOREN EISELEY

The Immense Journey
1957

Darwin's Century
1958

The Firmament of Time
1960

Francis Bacon and the Modern Dilemma
1962

The Mind as Nature
1962

The Unexpected Universe
1969

The Invisible Pyramid
1970

The Night Country
1971

LOREN EISELEY

Notes of an Alchemist

WITH DRAWINGS BY

Laszlo Kubinyi

CHARLES SCRIBNER'S SONS / NEW YORK

Copyright © 1972 Loren Eiseley

THIS BOOK PUBLISHED SIMULTANEOUSLY IN
THE UNITED STATES OF AMERICA AND IN CANADA—
COPYRIGHT UNDER THE BERNE CONVENTION

ALL RIGHTS RESERVED. NO PART OF THIS BOOK
MAY BE REPRODUCED IN ANY FORM WITHOUT
THE PERMISSION OF CHARLES SCRIBNER'S SONS.

B–12.72 (V)

PRINTED IN THE UNITED STATES OF AMERICA
Library of Congress Catalog Card Number 72-1902
SBN 684-13087-4 (cloth)

DEDICATED TO

MABEL LANGDON

MY WIFE OF MANY YEARS

IN APPRECIATION OF A DEVOTION

WHICH CANNOT BE SPOKEN ABOUT

SAVE TO SAY IT EXISTS

AS A FLOWER EXISTS

HAVING COME UNBIDDEN

INTO AN UNEXPECTED WORLD

TO A QUITE COMMON MAN

Contents

Preface

When I was a young man in college I wrote poetry. Other interests and the realities of the world I faced led me in the end to another vocation. I kept notebooks through the years, however, professional notebooks scrawled with scientific trivia and other matters of archaeological or biological interest. In these books an old habit of my student days persisted. I occasionally jotted a poem amidst the pages merely because, like a trade rat, I was making some kind of obscure interchange within my mind—keeping the ledger balanced as it were—an artifact for a poem or a poem for an artifact. Then there were animals I cherished and of which I have left some account in prose. My love for these creatures was recorded privately in poems which I no longer bothered to publish.

I have finally been persuaded, somewhat reluctantly, to release these poems. I say reluctantly not in the sense of being ashamed but rather because I have enjoyed them in secret for so long. Moreover, the austerities of the scientific profession leave most of us silent upon our inner lives. Now as I approach the time when I shall be leaving the academic world, *Notes of an Alchemist* will have to find its way alone.

The volume tells its own story, no doubt, of the eccentricities and diversities of my life—a kind of alchemy, in other words, by which a scientific man has transmuted for his personal pleasure the sharp images of his profession into something deeply subjective. Perhaps publishing at last in verse gives me a sense of release, of having unburdened myself of something that has haunted me at midnight. If the psychologists are right I should rest more easily hereafter. Whether my readers will feel the same, I cannot of course predict. They will have to practice their own alchemy, just as I have managed to vanish with the snow leopard. In all earnestness, I hope my friends will enjoy the book, but I am too timid to return through the snow to find out.

LOREN EISELEY

Notes of an Alchemist

NOTES OF AN ALCHEMIST

Crystals grow
        under fantastic pressures in the deep
                 crevices and confines of
the earth.
        They grow by fires,
             by water trickling slowly
in strange solutions
        from the walls of caverns.
They form
        in cubes, rectangles,
        tetrahedrons,
               they may have
their own peculiar axes and
        molecular arrangements
           but they,
      like life,
        like men,
          are twisted by
the places into which
        they come.

I have only
      to lift my hands
        to see
     the acid scars of old encounters.
            In my brain
as in the brains of all mankind
        distortions riot
and the serene
        quartz crystal of tomorrow is
most often marred
        by black ingredients
          caught blindly up,

but still
                no one knows surely why
                                specific crystals meet
in a specific order.
                Therefore we grasp
two things:
                that rarely
two slightly different substances will grow
                                even together
but the one added ingredient
                will transfigure
a colorless transparency
                to midnight blue
or build the rubies' fire.
                Further, we know
that if one grows a crystal
                it should lie
under the spell of its own fluid
                be
                kept in a cool cavern
                remote
                from any violence or
                                intrusion from the dust.

So we
        our wise men
                in their wildernesses
                        have sought
to charm to similar translucence
                the cloudy crystal of the mind.
We must then understand
                that order strives
against the unmitigated chaos lurking
along the convulsive backbone of the world.

Sometimes I think that we
          in varying degrees are grown
like the wild crystal,
           now inert,
now flashing red,
        but I
          within my surging molecules
by nature cling
        to that deep sapphire blue
          that marks the mind of one
long isolate
      who knows and does reflect
starred space and midnight,
        who conceives therefore
that out of order and disorder
         perpetually clashing and reclashing
come the worlds.
       Thus stands my study from the vials and furnaces
of universal earth. I leave it here
         for Heracleitus
if he comes again
      in the returnings of the Giant Year.

THE LOST PLATEAU

That lost plateau is a land of running water
drawn from invisible torrents in the sky,
crags, sinkholes, jumbled strata
                and always the water pouring
from cavern to cavern, basin to basin cascading
deeper and ever deeper till no rope, no ladder,
not even the hardiest of the climbers there
could reach rock bottom for there is no bottom,
only the sheer plunge of the water falling
into abysms that upset the ear
till voices cry out where there are no voices,
till tumult shouts and has a voice to speak,
but in that chaos like the primal chaos
in a still pool where cold stalactites drip
their solvent crystals into shapes uncertain
swims slowly, slowly a prophetic fish.
Here as though uncreate or held in waiting,
here in a darkness where all time has ceased,
swims a blind fish with barbels faintly tracing
upon those growing crystals runes so intricate
that only he who thundered in the torrents
or climbed the lightning's tree before it split
could read those cipherings or resolve their secrets
or tell who rules below the final pit.

THE CHANGELINGS

Fox masks, wolf masks, I try them on
as if I were a savage.
            Long ago I realized
                      from scratchings traced
                                on cave walls
or from dim ethnologies,
                from collections hidden
in musty storerooms or museum basements,
from phrenological attempts to see
                the beast in man,
how much of beast persisted.

Here was I
cursed by these foxes and their kin the wolves
to see them everywhere.

If my one-time friend the artist showed me a picture painted
of a closed garden
there was sure to be a fox who peered
from among the flowers,
a fox even the artist had not seen.
I have been cursed
for that as well, the artist crying he had not
seen the fox, he had not painted it,
but there it was
among the innocent flowers hiding
or among trees
or hidden
in a wheat field's tawny light.

Once seen, the artist
could not unsee it
though his brush was clean
of all intent;
the creature grew
just from my trembling finger tip until
by no subterfuge of the imagination could we
ignore it and forget.
For reasons plain my friend
chose to go elsewhere with his canvases.
Why blame him?
The faces sprang
from some
uncanny pleasurable perception.
I saw them in the boles of ancient trees,
in shadows dancing upon walls.
I am at last aware
that there exist

changelings
             born from a fourth dimension lurking
                   somewhere about
and I am one of these.   ' ' '

I see our blighted
                formalized
                pollution-filled
                   landscape of old cans,
                      bottles, and oil drums,
                         as if it held
ghostly potentials:
                      that the smiling fox
                         who was
                            lives in the shrubbery,
that the buffalo wolf still howls
                         upon the snowy hilltop
                            summoning
                            a nonexistent pack
                            for hunting lost
                            among old skulls
                            the prairie grasses cover.
My childhood was preoccupied with dreams
      of how to free all animals immured
                      in shabby local zoos,
                   in boxes foul,
                   in crates from which
                   the heaven-sweeping hawks
                   still scanned their wide dominions
                      helplessly.
So is it now. The fox, the wolf, the coyote,
                         the last
                      contenders against traps and poison
                            hold with grim teeth
                               slowly retreating
                      into waste lands where only coyotes run.

I am born of these,
              their changeling.
            Who first rocked
              my cradle
              or what wild thing left me
              upon my parents' doorstep
               is a mystery
                although
through this means I can see
              faces where faces are not
                      and I know
            a nature still
                  as time is still
                    beyond the reach of man.
You may search scarp and butte,
              read Indian pictographs
              on up-reared mesas,
              but you will not find
                  or trace
            more of me than is found
              in two poised ears
              behind my mother's picture
                  or
            on some rain-lashed night
              a voice that barks
               brief syllables
                may be
            at last my own.

THE FACE OF THE LION

The moth-eaten lion with shoe-button eyes
is lumpy by modern standards
                and his mane
scarcely restorable.
          I held him in my arms
                when I was small.
I held him when my parents quarreled
as they did often while
          I shrank away.
          My beast has come
down the long traverse of such years and travel
                  as have left outworn or lost
beds slept in, women loved, hall clocks that struck
              wrong hours,
            photographs
in years forgotten, notes, lovers' quarrels, dear God
                where go
our living hours,
          upon what windy ash heaps are they kept?
Down what sepulchral chambers must we creep
who seek the past?
          I who have dug through bones
and broken skulls and shards
              into the farther deeps
                rescind
such efforts now.
          I cannot practice
      the terrible archaeology of the brain
               nor plumb
one simple childhood thought. I want no light to shine
      into those depths forever
              but the lion

sits on the shelf above my desk
                                    and I,
                                    near-sighted now,
take comfort that he looks
                        forthright and bold
                    as when
my hands were small,
                    as when
my brain received him living,
                        something kind
                        where little kindness was.

The mirror tells me that my hair is grey
but the wild animist within my heart
refuses to acknowledge him a toy
given by someone long ago
                            forgotten.
No, no, the lion lives
                        and watches me
as I do him.
                    Should I forget
the hours in the blizzard dark,
                            the tears
spilled silent while I clutched his mane?
He is very quiet there upon the shelf,
as I am here, but we were silent
                            even then,
past words,
            past time.
                    We waited for the light
and fell asleep when no light ever came.

                            I do not
delude myself.
                The lion's face is slowly changing

into the face of death
   but when I lie down
       upon my pillow
         in the final hour
I shall lie quietly and clutch
     the remnants of his mane.
        It happens we have known
a greater dark together
      he and I.
I am not terrified
    if he has come
      wearing another guise.
To him the watcher I will trust my sleep,
     shoe-button eyes, the lion on the shelf.

THE INVISIBLE HORSEMAN

Bandit, revolutionary, hard rider, he crossed the border and raided
Columbus, New Mexico, in 1916.
I remember my father
bringing the papers.
After that the kids all over the West played
Pancho Villa for weeks
and were secretly pleased
when Pershing
never caught up.
Who wants the stern father
ever to catch up
to the hidden hideout,
the place where the
horses are tethered
for a fast getaway,
the hole in the wall.
But then the war came and we stretched black tarpaper
over frames of lath
and took off from the barn roof
to our later sorrow
and discomfiture
or ran about in the frames
maneuvering like bats
with the Lafayette Escadrille.
But all of that was even then too big for my sure comprehension,
too many orders,
discipline. I
had played Pancho Villa. I was the one horseman among us
who simply never stopped running
into maturity.
I never found
the hole in the wall;

I never found
Pancho Villa country
where you see the enemy first.
Still, I am the invisible horseman. I am among you,
breathless, but
still running.
You haven't caught me.
I am hiding in my own way,
My face only looks
mature.

MEN HAVE CHOSEN THE ICE

The elementals, the rock ribs, the cold root-nourishing stones
jut free through the cap rock.
                On this old farm
                      the dropped pebbles of the earlier ice
lie in windrows along the valley
            and the orange butterflies
dance over them the illusion of summer,
                  yellow and gold,
soft colors of the interglacials
                between ice ages past
and one oncoming.
          Throughout the hill land
            both can be felt blowing
              in the chill
              turn of the wind.
Soft butterfly summers
            dropped seeds and rich harvest
round the heart's full season
            but there is something
              in the contours of rock
                that always remembers
both seasons,
        the ice and the sun.

My people, the earlier ones,
             were like that.
They were here when all this was
                just territory.
Bullets and Sioux
         my grandfather said
always came with the spring.
             Still
              he did not hate

and from cavalry days
                knew the Indian sign
                              for peace
                                and could meet
warriors with grave dignity,
                  smoke a red pipe from the sacred quarries
                        miles away in Minnesota.

It was a wild land then
                    and the bison covered it
like a moving robe
              but the wheat
runs a far piece and is
                gold now,
grandfather used to say
                holding a hand to his eyes.
They were a pale fighting blue,
                not like mine,
                and my grandmother
in old photographs
            is either Indian or of the
                    black Scots who fought
                              at the Roman wall
but more likely
            with a touch of both.

They chose to remember in their own way the ice and the butterflies
                    and so
                    does their grandson
                    whose eyes are a compromise brown,
                            neither
of the ice
            nor the fierce black
                  of the buffalo people.
            I am
            the compromise:

I tell the tales
    in the Medicine Lodge;
I see the beginning and the end;
    I am both sides now;
I offer the pipe but know beforehand
    how few will take it.
Men have chosen the ice
    before its return.

THE STRIDERS

The water striders row on a film of water
                that can be broken by a beetle
                        who knows the secret of dissolving
                        the tension of the film.
Such chemistries reside
                in the night darkness of the molecule
                that seems to think.
Uncanny things
                hide in the water,
                        slide secretly
even into the living blood of man.
                The broken water film
plunges the rowing insect to his death
                but similar death can steal
through winding capillaries and the blood cells of man,
        the erythrocyte given a choice,
                        absorbing
            carbon monoxide
                        while treacherously forgetting
the oxygen that it was born to serve.

Man too is a strider over light and air
      but darkness waits below
        with more than just plain waiting.
Intricacies conceived
           within the substance of the universe
           can melt his living flesh
                but there is also
      directed against night
              this upward drive of things
that sets the strider rowing,
          that mostly holds the water film secure
          he dimples with his feet.

                    Man glides magnificently
upon a web of music and of light.
Something below contends against the dark.
                    and does not always win,
                              but wins enough
that music rises and a mocking bird
has his own repertoire of notes,
                    preserving others
                    of birds who sang once and were still.

These are the counters in a giant game
                    between two players playing in a secret
                              incredible dimension,
                              light and shade.
I think that man partakes
                    of both these gamesmen
                    and he plays
increasingly on one side, then the other, to his cost.
I also like the singing of the bird,
                              its bending
over the little nest that sends the song far on
                                        to other springs.
I tread most gently in this season; I
                    feel all the tension that the striders feel
                    and sense the gamesters in the molecule.
Knowing how suddenly a world can fall,
                    I always watch the striders in the spring.

SNOW LEOPARD

There is one animal who never stops
                 within the compass of the meanest cage.
The body stops perhaps but something travels
                 out and beyond—
it is the creature's eyes.
            Snow leopards are the grey
embodiment of blizzards
         and they travel
         with blizzards as a veil
            within their eyes.

He comes
up to the bars, grey-furred, with only
the faintest hint of the old
spotted pattern brought
up from green jungles
to Tibetan heights
in times before man was.
He knows his body
here must stop,
the strange thing is
his gaze just travels

on.

He is now one of the rarest of all creatures
on the earth;
not even
the Himalayan heights
are safe for him,
not any of his kind has late been seen.
He has
been trapped and transported.
He does not deign to see me,
his gaze is traveling
far outside his body,
he is hunting in a blizzard;
the blizzard is a veil for his eyes.
I wish I had those eyes,
that long-tailed supple body.
I would be away and hunting.
Snow would be always falling
I would never see the bars of cages,
my eyes would be traveling.
There would be always a blizzard.
A blizzard would be blowing;
snow beyond measure
would fill up my eyes.

I would never be seen. I would be invisible
    because of the blizzard I would carry,
      I would travel with the blizzard in my eyes.
At night I would be hearing
           as though they followed after
          but were my own
    the muffled footfalls
      of the leopard treading
   deep, deep and ever deeper
       into snow.

THE OLD ONES

The old gods are mosaics, *nahuales*, tricksters in all cultures,
laughing at man, at themselves, flinging the penis to
                                        become a snake
or the feathered snake a god, laughing, laughing
even while drinking blood, even while fitting
the cat's face to a man
                        beautiful, snarling, great art
expended upon a world now gone.
                        The Greeks in their strong sunlight
alone saw the gods as men though immortal;
                                        elsewhere, ranging
through fallen monuments, visions caught by
                        starving men on hilltops,
it is always
                the eagle, the great bison, coyote.
Sometimes we have fallen from the stars, sometimes
we have ascended through the seven caverns,
sometimes the bear aided us or was our father.

We are mosaics, forgive me, I think this wiser
than the emulation of Zeus, or the harsh-axed
                                        Vikings in their Valhalla.
I have found animals in me when I stroll in the forest.
I hesitate before a large dragonfly, I step
like a cat in the night, I have felt something
                lift along my neck
when a wolf howls. I could learn easily
to worship these, but not man projected
in every feature. For balance he needs to laugh,
he needs the vanished trickster behind the bush;
even if he fell from the stars, who was here to teach him?
The old ones, the old ones who knew and laughed and shared

thieves' knowledge of the sun,
                    how the beaver got his tail,
how to appease the game lords,
                    or marry the seal's daughter.
This is a very ordinary landscape but I feel in my body
                       the lost mosaic.
I am Lone Man and Snow Rabbit: the earth pleases me.
The wind has stolen my coat away,
                    my thoughts are becoming animals.
In this suddenly absurd landscape I find myself
               laughing, laughing.

ARROWHEAD

I found it there, ironically, in a graveyard
of my own kind, just flint, rain-washed, glistening, an arrowhead,
used by the painted bison hunters
for death—death on the snowy air.
The stone point had outlasted their autumns,
been dropped here, buried and cast up,
its flying purpose forgotten.
Gravely I lifted it in contemplation,
the serrated edge still menacing, purposeful,
the patina of age burnishing the worn stone,
death from the air unleashed and immanent
because of the craftsman's skill.
He had loved his instrument and so embellished it
that a man centuries away would finger the stone lovingly,
momentarily forgetting its purpose
in the greater glory of art—
a man from the two-cultured world
where the motivations are split,
and the scientist is not the poet,
and the poet never clasps like a workman with his hand
true death from the air.

Here leaning across the gravestone of one Milo
and his consort, Malvina,
I made the crossing, realized the beauty,
while the chipped edge, like glass,
drew blood from my hand.
I tasted the drop on impulse and the maker's voice
entered me, sang of the arrow,
and sang also
of the straight divinatory lines of mathematics, the space leaper,
first at the lion's heart,
but later, climbing by art and science together

past Saturn and Jupiter, the terrible ladder of space illimitable—
all shaped in the mind of the first artist in flint
                        who contained in his being
both the split worlds,
dreaming the deed in the stone, dreaming
dark in the single brain how space converges, how
this stone would pierce time
and be stopped nowhere.
Already it has fled from my hand,
climbing like the thundering Apollos in the moon's light,
hastening tomorrow.

THE SMALL DEATHS

They say the Oregon trail
        cost a man a mile,
          they say the same
for laying the first transcontinental rails,
            I suppose it was that way
              on the Erie canal
                and even skyscrapers:
they estimate a man per floor up there
            on the high iron.
      In a grove of trees out west
      I found a little huddle of gravestones
          once in a blizzard,
all broken, names gone
        into the pounding sleet,
           no trace
of a settlement,
       but somebody must
        have set the stones;
         somebody
knew about it once and the story
       is always old and sad.
      I have even found those little wooden
           crosses
that last awhile in the Sonoran desert
      Ah, *falsos amigos,* are they not
everywhere?
The great kings have their pyramids and barrows
          to break time like a wave,
their cups and helmet plates still shine,
       but I
have this pain for the small deaths.
      I remember Snippet
        the cat who came from Eden,

must have because of lovingness,
                    trapped and throttled by a basset hound
in its own small runway:
        evidence it had expected
                    and not received
the gentleness of the world.
                    Whenever willows bud in the spring
where Snippet lies buried
the pain of the little deaths comes back to me:
                        those no one remembers
long ago   yesterday   today   and tomorrow.

I try to remember
        as though I could bend time to some purpose,
                                restore justice,
                            but no,
there are only this year's willows, Snippet
                    easily to be pulled up by another owner
uncaring.
            Falsos amigos,
                they had that phrase in Sonora,
                        a hard land
                                and they placed it
                over the innocent who died untimely.

Some are doomed to remember the little deaths
                    never to be undone.
I remember Snippet
                and the crosses in the sands of Sonora,
                    never anything clear of the great.

THE BEAVER

A beaver's skull is something not many people see any more,
or would recognize, since mostly
gone with the mountain men or Coronado's armor.
I found it there on the north bank of the Kaw
              hunched down with all its bones,
like little pebbles, sleeping around it,
                        sleeping
what sleep I scarcely know,
                but I gathered them,
and the huge orange-colored incisors,
                              the tree splitters,
I reset in the jaw.

Like a foiled magician appreciating puzzles
                            but impotent to create
I had the parts but the watch spring
                        eluded me.
So I boxed them,
The weathered grey bones after many journeys
                            and uncertain years
lying here on my desk.

It is man who is the popular animal now
                but just looking at him one is never sure
                      for what he was framed
or if chance somehow
                obscured the intention.
There is no certainty,
                  but in this old skull,
                  this puzzle from the bed
of a prairie river,
                there is intention
                in a way not easily found.

He knew something,
            kept in his way a continent
                        from sliding
into the sea.
You have to know the way the ear canals
                        cased in bone
spring up and out from the flat skull—
                all those little signs
of the perfectly adapted water dweller and pond planner
                                    extraordinary,
                the kind of thing
nature whispers in thickets
                before moonrise,
scholars not hearing.

I think something taught him in the intricate chain of the genes.
You have only to look at the bone
to feel your flesh crawl,
                but mystery
brings nothing back.
            I remember only the silence
            of the river where I found him.
One leaf fell
            and a one-dimensional bird
laughed from a tree.
                Teleology they say
is out of fashion
                but the beaver was here
before the dam builders,
                old orange tooth
and the laugh of the one-dimensional bird
summarizing confusion.

FLIGHT 857

Nosing in through a blizzard over Denver
                    at thirty thousand feet
I think what the earth covers at Lindenmeier there far away to the
                                        north—
those men we never found
                  of ten millennia ago
                      but still
                finding the heavy-headed
                beasts of the gone time, finding
                in the end
      how short one's own existence,
                      one pauses.

I suppose, beyond the low clouds and the snowfields,
       lie the marks of the trenches where forty years ago we dug
      and we found them, found
          the Ice Age long-horned bison,
            the deadly point buried still
              in the massive vertebra.

We proved something;
     they write about it in books now
         but that lost doorway of snow
       through which the hunters were enticed to venture
       will eventually
          close behind us also.
Staring north through the falling flakes,
               the hills invisible,
    I think just once of the moment
     when the fluted chalcedony
   dropped into my hand
         but really
        I know now
it should never have been resurrected
any more than these wheels and wings and electronic voices
       should ever again be lifted
           from oblivion.

I hope they do not find us:
       the point should remain in the vertebra,
       the offering by the dead child in the cave,
       the pterodactyl in the slate,
       the poet in the lost book,
       the singer as song in the grass.
Why must we usurp
       the autumn leaf's prerogative
       or the cancellations of running water
       or the erasures of the dust?

Like the hunters, we will leave deadly slivers of glass
                    where they left flint,
                    the metal will oxidize.
We will be dangerous if found
                    by anything wiser
                    than a field mouse.
I hope he will take it upon himself to betray no secrets
                    nor resurrect even
                    that little artifact
                        the mousetrap
                        lest it be
                            disastrously reactivated.
It would take a glacier to pulverize us completely to chalk dust
                    but even at Lindenmeier
            the hunters had the grace to tiptoe
                    away with the last mammoth.
We never found them,

                    only their flints.
So be it forever

                    with us
and all those who come after.
                    Amen.

THE SANDBURS SAY NO

Along the edge of the airfield between the jet blasts
from ascending bombers,
low life, the tougher
seeds from the far Cretaceous, surreptitiously test the concrete,
with the old mindlessness
sow crevices and wait.

The blue devil's darning needles
dance their mating ecstasy across the bombing targets—
nature's archaic first streamlining,
still magnificent in a small way but useless,
the gun ships deadlier, more purposeful, but

the sandburs say no, the sandburs
are older, the sandburs
toughen the seed containers, the life bombs,
against thermite, napalm, nerve gas. The sandburs
like spendthrift governments pack the little brown
                              bullets and send them
out on each wind.

Each season they test the concrete and the bomber's targets.
The explosions are soundless but the stone fractures.
The sandburs say no with the life bombs,
the sandburs say no.

THE FIGURE IN THE STONE

Mud spattered, grimed with sweat, upon my door
he beat a loud tattoo
            and when I opened
held in his hand a precious object there—
to him at least most precious.
                   When I stood
upon my threshold in a mild surprise
he asked at once:
               "You are the fellow
                         digging,
the fellow with the bones,
            the man who knows
                    old things?"
"Well you see," I countered, "I am bothered
with bones and stones, it's true, but there are things
we know and some we don't.
              What is it? who are you?"
"I'm from down there," he answered,
           "where we're digging
the subway tunnel,"
        and I knew he looked
sprung from the clay
        of glacial sediments and sand.
"It's a rock," he said, and showed a pebble eagerly.
"You can see a woman,
         you can see
a woman carved in it, look at the lines."
He let me take the stone reluctantly.
His thumbnail there was huge.
I turned a desk light on and tried my best.
I washed it, magnified it, turned it
        while he tried to show

meanwhile just where the figure lay.
                                        There were
                      scratches the moving ice had
one time made, completely natural
                      and nothing more.
                              "I think you are mistaken, sir," I said,
trying to explain what ice could do
when once it marched.
                      That age of shadow grew
and menaced me within the room.
                      "It *is* a woman," he protested loudly.
                                        His shoulders
bulked like a bear, a savage,
                              and a true believer
conjured
              up from the farther reaches of dead time.
"I tell you that I know and you can see."
I saw it was an icon
                      and an object
such as men cherished in lost caves when only
              the sacred mothers of the tribe
                              were real.

"It is dark," I said appeasing, "down where
                              you've been working.
Maybe you've seen what can't be seen up here.
We only see what each of us can see, no more.
Take it if you wish,
                      preserve it, say that no one
except yourself perhaps can be so sure."
                      He took it like a trusting child,
the bear grown suddenly
                      gentle again.
                              He wrapped it close away
in his wet jacket.

When I let him out I touched his shoulder.
"Take care of it," I warned, "remember only you can see it clearly."
He listened as though he heard a thing behind me,
turned and went.
        Always, I thought,
           leaning against the door, this inner barrier,
always the inscrutable rubric growing fainter
from mind to mind that strives to read the world.
We tried to climb with masks
                back into the shape of animals;
                      we failed.

We tried
the ever-fecund mothers,
        the returning cycles
            of many
unreturning gods.
        What is there lies
down in the subways that we have not seen?
What new wild hand is scrawling on the walls
the approaching mammoth and the giant bear?
Softly I turned and looked outside the window
into a rain that never ceased to fall
on men still splotched with clay.

FROM US WITHOUT SINGING

The dead bird in the back yard under the spruce tree
I have passed many days now while slowly
all the ugly innocent necessary work of nature
is carried on by beetles, ants, blowflies—
all those immediate molecular transpositions
                            that ensure
the endless procession of pine needles, new eggs,
new birds and in their turn
new deaths.
            I was born in cyclone time, raised out of
glacial dust;
            I ought to know
something about origins and transformations
                        having been once a crawling
glacier and an anticyclone.
                        There are those seemingly content with
                            the flow of things
but I in that old cellar that filled with flood water
                        every spring,
I hated it as a child when they killed
                        the lime-green mud puppies
thinking they were poison, thinking
they had no right to be what they were.
                        I do not understand very well
where thought goes, I resent the slow
disarticulation of this summer bird and his own
particular eye, to be a transplant
                    in a beetle's stomach.
I am bound like this bird
                to my own carcass, I
love this year's light,
                    the music in his, my mind.

I do not say like the poets,
                watching the last feather of this
                        small creature
blow away into dust,
                        he has rejoined the chain,
do not grieve,
                he has reentered the wheel.
I want to know
                where thought is restored
and memory under this one summer's sun.
                        It does not please me
that the individual mud puppies
                        are gone from the farm cellar,
that there is a desiccated hawk nailed on the barn wall.
It does not please me,
                the lost song of this bird under the spruce tree,
its last recognizable feather
    reentering the wheel of existence is no comfort.
I remember too many of these deaths.
                I want to know where thought goes
in the turning wheel and where enters
                the touched hand at midnight.
Oh yes,
        I came out of the wheel
                but if I must reenter
give me   give me
                        the crawling glacier in its continental miles,
                        give me once more the dust cloud,
                        the anticyclone, my father, screaming
from the marching ice front.
                By god if I must reenter,
let it be on the scale of my hatred,
let me crawl with boulders like the diamonds on a snake's back,
let me coil ice and utter silence,
                if there can be no thought,
halfway around the world.

Small bird so pitifully disassembled
I make you a promise: reentering the wheel
        they shall hear from us without singing;
there is another way to speak from the cloud,
            to bring down the everlasting sleet.

THE HIGH PLAINS

I found the pink catlinite bowl of an Indian pipe
   and an iron arrowhead

      once in the middle of a road in Kansas.
I suppose the road graders had cut through a house pit,
but this is the way

    one culture tumbles into another.

In the dust-bowl days
    when the soil was mostly

        traveling

         by air

you could find lying mixed on the hardpan
                              antique barbed wire,
                              a branding iron from Texas,
                              a fragment of
                                whiskey jug,
                              shards of Indian pottery,
                                mammoth teeth,
                                and flint knives.
The debris covered ten thousand years and it wasn't much,
                              considering the time,
                                  nor was it easy
                              to measure the intervals
                                from one chipped stone
                                    to another.
They had all sifted down from their previous levels as the wind blew
                              the earth away
                              and on the hardpan
                              they huddled together,
                              the artifacts of the literate
                              and the illiterate,
                              not too dissimilar
                              in final purpose.
Looking on there one saw everything, including one's self,
                                        in final perspective.
                              Five hundred human generations
                              leave very little.
                              On the high plains
                              the soft stuff goes first
                              and that includes
                                  man.

WHITE NIGHT

In those long desert nights
             on the playas,
                      the dead lake beds
that used to be fed
                      from snow water
before the glaciers
                      died in the far-off mountains,
I used to watch
                      the constellations
                               turning all night
                                        around the horizon
                      and think
of great angular distances,
                      of light-years
compressed in my head.
                      I think it must have been there
                      between the sand dunes
where everything human
             was reduced to stones
                               polished
             by a million years of wind
that I forgot how it was to sleep.

Now the geometry of space has widened
             beyond my skull's capacity.
I am too old
             to sleep on the ground,
             too old
                      to gather flints that had just as well
                      be left lying
                               for another age.

I sit against a rock.
                    It is easier now
                          for
            my mind follows the night wind
            over dunes and pinnacles.
            I can hear it whisper
                each time more softly
that there is no need
                          to come back,
                          that I myself am the wind
                          so long whispering
                          that our identities
                          are both cast in doubt.

Wind and thought,
                        they both blow
                    over immeasurable distances;
        they drop and lose things
                                or nudge
            something better left buried
                                    out of the sand;
            then they cry
                        away over deserts
                                        to do it again
not caring.

I think that the mind remembers
                            more than the wind.
Though I am old
                I shall keep this difference
                    but for me
            it is necessary to be wakeful
            holding the broken shards together
                    a little while
                seeing what Plato saw in the eidos,

the forms,
                taking a final pleasure
            in what the wind
            can neither proclaim
                nor destroy.
The flint knife on the playa,
                though singular,
                            survives
and is now an eidolon
            shaped in the darkness of the
                    beginning years.
The wind has buried and unburied it
                for ages;
it is still what it is.
Remember this when you write the notes
                of a song.
Intend it for travel
                for light-year distances.

NOT TIME CALENDRICAL

I have thrown memory away on careless things,
                              remembered
how it was with me when I lay ill
                              in the den of my books
sleepless and tried to make
                              a poem of the parking lot,
how when someone flushed a lavatory
                              far off
                                        upstairs
                                                  in another apartment
                                        and the drain
told me some troubled sleeper did not sleep,

I felt affection
for that unknown person who looked out upon a scene
as bleak as I did
and perhaps had wept.
These, these at last are memory,
not time calendrical, but all
we did not will to hold
or did not want.
You understand?
The thing done in unthinking childhood
not ever to be forgotten,
the struck animal that cried
there by the road
and goes on crying
somewhere in the brain,
so here
the leaving of this place, four walls in which a quarter-
century has passed,
wakes all these clocks I did not will to wake,
the toy turtle that wags his head,
the books that must be sold
before I die,
the coral no one wants,
the beaver skull
from a lost prairie
and another time.
All, all is ending here.
I watch the lights
through tesselated towers far away.

This is another land than time; it is
a series of eternities
so long as mind
holds to its orbit.
I am that I am.
I did not will

the notes on the piano that resound
when all the house is quiet;
I did not will
the loneliness that follows room to room,
the bird upon the windowsill
that I must feed—
or must I?
Did my own will create
that which I suffer from?
I am that which came
from a far province
and another dust.
I beseech
return into a silence and sufficient ending.
But still not yet, not now.
These things are I;
I loved them. I am perishable as they are, but I know
that when they go this entity myself
no longer has a center.
Say that I
seek to defend these things so long as memory lasts
and memory is
the mortal enemy of time that flows.
The turtle and the seed, the ancient sword,
the coral from the blue depths of the sea,
I hold them all as a great king might hold
his last beleaguered castle and its treasures
against the ram and battering ax of night.
Say that I died upon the battlements. Say that flame
consumed these treasures that were not supinely yielded.
Say that a world died with me and be done.

THE BLIZZARD

He was one of those physiological misfits, poor in countenance,
    weak before his time,
        a poor teacher
           inept in human relations,
           not really knowing
               how to speak to others,
                    in the end retired early
because students objected and no one could find him useful.

Afterwards I used to see him on the same train
               in the mornings,
carrying little piles of books from the library,
dozing in the Club
               and repeating without purpose
or wife to divert him
               the routine of an academic day.
Many end thus, for the world is pitiless
        and to bores and the prematurely senile
               more pitiless still.

Why do I remember this grey faceless man with the
                    threadbare overcoat,
remember him when the bright, the able, the young
    have their own unpredictable way of perishing
                  in the harsh sunlight of spring?

I think it must have been because of the blizzard,
             the worst in years, wind lashing
snow in one's face, snow flying so thick one
             could hardly see
at the street corners, the blast rising
          over rocking signs and crashing shutters,
the drifts beginning to efface the cars.

Oh yes, I was out in it by chance,
                    being myself
a creature of snowfalls,
                         an observer, in a way, of
that strange violence which can strike from the open sky.

I was alone save for one other man on the street.
I saw him through the haze of the snow flakes
                    staggering a little in the clutch
                              of the wind.
He had left the bookstore and was headed—
where was he headed?
          who knows?
          I saw him sit down to gain breath at a
                              cornerstone;
                         he was
gasping heavily, his face unnaturally red.
                    I lingered
behind the curtain of snow.
          He saw me and arose unsteadily—
                    it was quite evident
as always
               he wanted no one,
no speech, no arm, no elbow, no assistance.
                    I followed a few paces but he left me,
                         turned where I had no reason to follow,
                         bent double against the storm and vanished.

What should I have done? Led him like an animal to
                    shelter—oh no.
I do not think that it was warmth he was seeking.
Snow is a beautiful white way into death,
               more beautiful, I think, than spring.
I rarely read the obituaries, but I did not see him
                              thereafter.
I shall only remember the one glance from his eyes

and the grey indeterminate shape that was his life
                     as it slipped silently away
                                    into the storm.
It may be it was for this he had waited, had
                             chosen just once
                          his proper exit.
I am a student of nightfall, I claim no other profession.
I stood a long time in the street while the snow covered me—
                                this is
                how I remember him better, perhaps,
                         than all others.

MAGIC

Magic, an anthropologist once said,
        simply was from the beginning.
                It was never
created or invented.
          It travels across time
because of the treacherous imponderables
          like death
with which man has to cope.

Malinowski wrote of man and of human concerns
                   and evasions, but I
have remembered that magic
          was said to be from the beginning,
the beginning left undefined.
        I have lived much among animals
in a small way,
       bartering with food for information,
          trying to discern
whether the bright flame in the mind of man
      is at all matched
          in fur or feather,
        for I
love forms beyond my own
      and regret the borders between us.

We always feed our cardinal family at the
            kitchen window.
It took them a long time to understand this
       and to come
          regularly
       but now
more than one generation
      has lived here and they know

the entire ritual—
                    the window lifted,
the placing of seeds,
                    the withdrawal of hands,
                         the window closed,
the prudent wait before coming.
                    Even the wild ones will approach doubtfully
following their mates' example.
                                   Not magic perhaps but a kind of
                                   unspoken learning.
                                             Still
they have problems like man.
                              Squirrels come,
                              pigeons interfere,
                              and the cardinals
are withdrawn solitary aristocrats.
                         They do not like to eat
                                             squabbling
                                                  at table.

Like any old émigré
                         I try to help them but time defeats me
                         with a hundred sparrows.
Yesterday moving about in my den I discovered
                              the pair of cardinals
sitting on a windowledge where sunflower seed
                              never grows
                              and the window
is far from the source of food
                         and never opened.
                              It was evident
they had detected movement inside
                         and perhaps the strange
                              giving animal
could be persuaded to change his habits if they perched there.
                    I did what I could.

I went back to the kitchen. I performed the ritual
                    and they came in the old way.

                    Like man they
                        have problems;
                        like man, what works
                        may work again.
This is the root of magic
                and science,
                        life's response to
                                uncertainties—
                if a thing works
                    you try it
                    and try once more
                    and again
                    until
                    you are absolutely sure
                    it will never work,
                    then try it once more.
                    That is magic,
                    and animals and people
                    live or die
                    by the uncertainties.

I shall never forget the first redbird
                    to come to our house.
                    Birds differ like men
                        and he
                    was very different
                        and very beautiful.
In the morning—
                    and it worked because I am
                    a dawn riser—
he would fly back and forth along the whole
                    tier of windows
                    crying his morning song

telegraphing in quick clicks his hunger,
until I fed him.
He was, I think, practicing vocal magic
that mostly worked.
He was
the most brilliant cardinal that ever came to us,
the most responsive.
Somewhere in a few weeks he met with an accident
and the nest was deserted.

Magic runs to the beginnings of life because
life is a gift and uncertain.
Both I and the bird practiced magic and were
beginning to pass a mutual threshold.
In the mornings now I remember.
I feed the birds
but nothing like him
ever came again
I was the sorcerer's apprentice for a little while. I am powerless
without him.
I learned from him also how little magic can do
to stave off death
but this does not seem
the whole lesson.
I continue to feed the birds. I wait for another
friendly magician.
He convinced me
we were on the same path.
Even if no one comes
I am glad
that he made his magic work for a little while.
This is something
not given to many of us.
I miss him.
He made me happy
and is not that a kind of magic?

It is years now
but I
still lie awake and listen
in the mornings.

How does a man say to his fellows
he has been enchanted
by a bird?

Paulfrye

THE LAST BUTTERFLY

There is a sweet-smelling bush in the front yard,

                               nameless;

            a man now dead,

                one of those green-thumb people who know

            strange plants with which

                        esoteric nurseries

like the world

            are stocked

bought and planted it there.

It may be from the Andes
                    or Tibet
                    or some other
                    less notable place.
It has a unique fragrance
                    given to the air
          from an inconspicuous
                              yellow flower
                    but I cherish it
each spring and watch
                    less for itself perhaps
than because
                    a beautiful swallowtail butterfly
                    comes from far off
                              to sip at the blossoms.

You must understand they are rare
                    in this city now,
                              these creatures of a single season
                    whom I always think of
because of the one butterfly
                    on my solitary bush
as one immortal,
                    appearing   disappearing
                              with the golden seasons,
                                        but essentially
one immortal
                    entering the winter dark
                              returning, always returning
                              to the single
                              summer plant in the world.

The world is a cone
                    converging from childhood where
these creatures were about me,

where I knew of the
pupating darkness of the
sphinx moths
beneath the potato plants
in October
or
the golden chrysalids
hanging hidden
in the winter storms,
the resurrection
in the spring,
the aimless drifting
flitting
elusive
high over backyards
and in meadows
black, gold, yellow,
dancing,
the essence of summer and
sunlight eternal.

I hold it now
in age
by means of
the last tiger swallowtail.
There is only one
each summer
slowly moving
his delicate wings,
sipping
in the golden bush.
I try to touch
just delicately
his wing—
he will not allow me,

           he is
               always
up and gone
         into a spring
                    far off
beyond my reach.

THE WHITE PYTHON

I sometimes dream of death as a huge white python
        lying coiled in crisp brown leaves
                                on the path where nothing comes
save I, in this dream,
        along this gallery forest where only the leaves rustle
        and the wind sighs and there are far-off drums
from native villages beyond in the sullen mountains,
        but on the path itself nothing at all has stirred
        for a summer's day, no flower has fallen, nothing
has told of its existence or of mine. My footsteps
        are lost in the whisper of leaves until I see
that woman of my youth on the dark horse riding
        before me as she rode once long ago
        down another aisle, among the flickering trees,
        in another country where galloping did not help me
        and the sand in the horse's hoofprints sifted back.
So is it here, except that suddenly
        after that face eternally young has passed
        and the hoofbeats sound and are gone upon the air,
death, the huge white python, rears upward from the path
        with eyes of obsidian black, while into them,
        those imperturbable pupils, depth within depth, I see receding
        down another aisle in another country, the horse
        and its fair rider. Pursuit
        is ended here, leaving me in the gallery forest
        leaving me in the leaves already fallen,
        leaving me to the sere clash of the palms that quiver in my head.
I shall stare, I know, into black obsidian forever
        seeing the rider vanish and not vanish.
The drums will sound once more in the sullen mountains;
the huge upreared white serpent will hold me close ensorcelled
        as eye to eye with him I forget

how the beautiful rider passed
                    wherever it was she passed me
and how it was I searched before sleep found me
the seeker and the sought in that ophidian eyeball fading
        into a night so black there could be no regret.

THE CABIN

Rough hewn, square logged.

As we rode up, a sand dune was just beginning
to swallow the far side.

The cabin lay on the edge of nowhere
abandoned in cattle country that a nester

had tried to farm unsuccessfully,
or been shot, or run off.

I could never find it again.

Probably
the big dune has covered it by now

and stabilized in the wet years.

Perhaps the same things
are still lying on the floor
with the grass and the hill
                overhead.
I remember seeing the washpan
                        with cast-iron handles
                        hanging under the eaves.
It gave me a fey sense of time relived, I
cried to the others, my companions,
                look, it's the kind my folks used
                when I was a little boy,
                look! and someone
                        laughed.
Inside there was nothing much:
                        a long-laced, woman's shoe—
                        my god what use did she
                                have for it there—
                        a Sears Roebuck catalogue
                                of 1900,
                        and blowing ceaselessly
                                upon the floor
a newspaper with an almost modern lead:
                        Great Japanese Naval Victory
                                Russian Fleet
                                Annihilated at
                                Tsushima Strait.

Teddy Roosevelt was president.
                It was 1905.
                In the cabin
                a clock had stopped,
                that was all.

Where was the woman who left
                one lady's shoe
                in cow country?

Where was the man who left dozens of
                      delicately tapered beer bottles
            in the storm cellar?
They are high-priced in Philadelphia now,
                they are antiques.
We did not touch anything, a spell held us:
                 the beginning of the modern world,
              the guns that led to
                    Pearl Harbor,
          naval victories
              blowing on the floor
                of the last frontier cabin,
              time so slow
                so fast.
We tiptoed away.
               The cabin is surely
           under the dunes now,
           swallowed,
            time stopped at 1905.

They left the washpan hanging
                 on a nail under the eaves.
        I wonder where they went
                    or whether
            they were already sleeping
             somewhere near us.
People are incalculable in their departures.
          I have someone's Colt revolver and a dice box
          but no address.
It will be so with us
          far off in a cabin of our own.
The riders in the yard will say
            the clock stopped
           and ride off laughing
          into another century.

Think of us, please. We shall be
nameless,
lonely.
There will be no one to explain why we forgot the washbasin
or one shoe on the floor.
We will appear odd, yet there was
possibly a reason.
We were
like you.
Remember us. This is all that is left.

THE LAST DAYS

A pheasant came into my apartment yard Sunday

                                     and headed straight

for the wall of the parking lot

                         over which he presently vanished.

His compass was wrong I am sure

       and he probably ended

       in a cooking pot

             for he was

       pointed in the wrong direction

               but then I get these doubts.

Heracleitus once said

           polemos . . .

war and Zeus are the same.

       A long way off to be thinking

       what I am thinking

       but the reports come in.

My den is a command post,

          a suburban fire center.

One fox seen in the neighbors' garden,

        a tiger swallowtail

        by god in spite of DDT

        sipping flowers by the window—

        not many in the springs now.

     The clockface sunflowers

you wouldn't believe don't get pollinated because

           the pollinators are mostly gone

           but last night

a buck deer was seen close in on route 30;

           they didn't get him but he was headed,

                        so they say,
straight toward the city.

                    I sometimes see flowers
inclining that way;
                I sometimes see
                plants growing on boxcars.
There are skunks here.
                Once I caught
                            a bat in the hallway
                            but turned it loose
                            against better judgment.
Polemos, war—I tell you
        they keep coming, keep coming,
raccoons, foxes, butterflies.
        I heard a chipmunk whistle
in the drain pipe.
                They lose, why do they have to keep
                        coming?

The city is ours
                I think,
                        but less certain now.
Resolved: I should not release prisoners.
                That golden butterfly
                            was beautiful.
                I am not good with a flit gun.
Hear this: they keep coming, woodchucks, box turtles,
            and they say cougars
have returned to the East coast.
            I am alone here. I consider Heracleitus.
He said *Polemos* and God were the same.
            If so we've had it;
                if it takes them
                a long march and the casualties

I see in the road,
                    if it takes them ten thousand
                    or tens of thousands
                    in years,
                              we've had it,
Polemos and Zeus: the birds sit on the wires
                              watching us.

Sometimes I think of defecting:
                    I have begun to hear
                              trees in the night;
                    I wander around too much
                              and need replacements.
Animals are beginning to look better
                    than my own kind;
I request transfer.
                    Sometimes I think they are talking.
                    My cat is talking
                              but I don't quite hear.

I should not have read Heracleitus: seditious literature.
Transfer is advisable.
                    I am beginning to comprehend . . . what? Never mind.
                    A war is a war. I like this post better
                              than the city but
                    I will not kill butterflies
                              and I cannot see foxes any more.
                    Perhaps it is my eyes in the night
                              or is it my face
                                   that is slowly changing?
                    I will no longer
                              look into mirrors.

THE OLMECA

Men recoil from them, these heads of ponderous stone.
If one must see them, one should see them as they lie
bodiless, pocked with green lichens, touched
                         with yellow leprosy like the rain forest.
Indestructible, not carved to be moved, only to stare
                         upward into a sky
not present, waiting, the brutal faces made to be brutal, no sigh
has touched them, no moan whispered here since they were made.
How else is time outfaced? I tell you whoever made them
made them brutal, made them to be bowled against the centuries,
made them to endure roots, the coil of the bushmaster
sunning his venomous head on man's creations.

                Mark
the sky is not present yet, waiting, the sky
these heads are timed for.
                  Lightning for three millennia
has crashed over them, fungi have mottled their features,
foot-long centipedes have tested their poisonous grip on these faces
and been repelled. The features are brutal.
Some mathematical priest passing his calculations
               thrice through the fire knew how the faces
must be made. They lie here bodiless, waiting
a sky not present yet.
                In the buried ruins someone has unearthed
                    a laughing jaguar
of exquisite workmanship, but not very human. It smiles
toward a sky not present yet, not ours, but a little beyond us.

THE BATS

I well remember when a fallen leaf

      bounced up and hissed at me.

It was just a bat

   downed in an autumn rainstorm,

helpless because

    it needed to climb upward on some tree

and could not take to air from where it lay.

     Still, it had spat

at my descending foot

    and saved itself,

     for in the end

I gathered it

   safe in the dry fold of a magazine

and placed it

   where its small twilight world

could be reentered on a tattered wing

that always fell

   through darkness

     then reversed its fall

to climb secretive on the winds of night.

Bats also find their way through caves and moonlit steeples.

They have been persecuted in fanatic years

as succubi or devil's children, familiars

   of that old world we fear

because we cannot see

    by sonic clicks and echoes

but only by our eyes.

    Once in an ancient church in Mexico

I heard faint squeaks and whimperings

    behind a sacred painting.

When I lifted

   the picture frame just far enough I saw

a row of eerie faces with enormous ears
tilted in my direction.
                            One took off
and flew into the dim light of the nave
his shadow floating on the stones below.
The priest whom I accompanied shrugged and said
Los muertos—
                    we do not really care
                                to trouble them, *señor,*
they have their own ways,
                                and we do not know
from whence they come.
                                They shelter here with us
among the saints. Would you not say,
amigo, this itself suggests
                        what is permitted
of a Christian man,
                        a creature fallen?
Is it not a sign
                from him who reigns above?

I raised my eyes most dubiously and thought
I saw a moment's mockery in that wise
                                time-haunted face.
My thoughts themselves appeared to take on shape,
to dip and hover in waste glades or run
into each barred loft and crevice of the world.
Father, I said, these are, and we ourselves may be,
fragments of the original creation that was done
upon the seventh day,
                        but only fragments,
                            therefore it is we fly
by shapes of thought or upon leathern wings to find
what's lost in each of us.
Small brother bat, the autumn leaf, once tested
what had been lost and now is found in me.

We set the picture in its place and wandered
in our own thoughts.
                              To me there came
in the solemnities of that great church
                    built by descendants of conquistadors
hissings of leaves, snappings of owls' beaks,
                              unbearable blank stares
of Himalayan leopards behind bars.
                    All, all are part
          of a fractured theology that God implants
within such brains as ours and leaves
                              the question open how to salvage
these bits and pieces of
          the natural world that is not natural
                    but a queer event created
in minds still queerer.
                    So we poke and pry
          into the atom's heart, triangulate
all visible stars
                    but still we cannot find
the serene center, but only void, void
                    across the light-years,
only the crackle of
                    intolerable flames
in the heart's darkness, as in spiral nebulae and suns
that shine invisible unless their light should touch
beyond the galaxies such eyes as ours.

                    Oh God forgive us doubts,
within this fallen fractionated world of night's creation bring
all brown leaves to the universal leaf,
                              all tigers, yellow-eyed,
to where the tiger is,
                    and to men in torment bring
the single face that has not come again
                    in all Jerusalem's years.

[87]

Bring at last dark to the unstirred dark that was
before creation, bring
                    light to its beginnings,
bring all things
                    back to what reigned before creation was.
This is the search of man, this is the pity found
within the protest of an autumn leaf that hissed and beat
against my footstep on a sidewalk long ago
                    in the poor environs of a prairie town.

Bring us then to where the heart of man may rest
                before the torrent of the universal fall
                    diverged its particles—
                                    these eyes that shine
unwinking in the night and then are gone,
                            the teeth that tear
because there is no other hope for them
                            in present nature;
bring us to
                the uncreated Adam;
                        bring us back
beyond the light-years
                    into the light that was
before this curving light that never ceases
upon itself to run, but above all
                        bring us
to where bats, leaves, and men no longer know themselves
the solitary occupants of night
                        but rather
the tenants of a Garden that must be because
minds of His mind conceived of it although
they choose to call it universal myth,
                    thus naming on the night
                                what was
before inception.

Return the apple
to the unshaken bough
while each of us,
serpent and Eve and Adam and the creatures,
gaze steadily upon its timeless surface as it was
before one bite was taken.
Give us
not night
but peace,
the peace that long ago was said to pass
beyond our human understanding.
Give it to all your creatures,
for we too are a part of them as they of us
entwined in one great whole that cannot keep
the mind from terror so long as one lost leaf
upon the pavement struggles within its solitude to rise.

THE HAND AX

I picked it out of a gravel bed
        far up in a badland canyon
many years ago;
                it is with me still,
a great stone pebble
            pounded into a point
                    that resembles
the tools of the earlier ice,
            the base
                harsh and unworked
for the powerful hand that once held it.

Professionals from Africa
            have fondled it and said to me
              you picked it up of course
                  somewhere
near the Rift or on the
            high veldt.
But no,
      it is from some lost horizon
early or late in the Americas.
           When I found it
              the stone
            had been tumbled by freshets
              too far to trace,
rolled and pounded onward
            in the traverse of years.
Like words I thought,
              like our words
tumbling down the centuries
            over the rough tongues of men
through torrents murky
            or flashing white water,

obscene
       or beautiful
            but lying lost in the end
wherever it is
         that words
                like stones
stop rolling and die,
          knocked out of shape perhaps
on the coarse gravel of another tongue
        or taking some other meaning
not given to stones
          before they die.
Barbaralexis
        someone called it
in another century
        but this flint ax
will not alter
form like the old affectionate word for elf child, changeling,
         transformed
            slowly
              to oaf
                 in a bleaker time.
The ax may have been out of fashion
         a hundred millennia
           but you can still
recognize its true purpose.

         I wish it were possible
to fix a word between us
         which would last in the torrent
longer than slivers of bone,
        and that someone
           picking it up
wherever it is that words
          finally are tossed on the stream banks
           would say

this was once used

        in the old high senses of love,

           out of use now perhaps

but a good word

           of proud meaning;

it has come a long way down,

           been battered, but lasted,

           is recognizable.

Take it home,

        say it just once.

It has a good sound still,

like the feel of the ax now

           held in my hand.

THE CARDINALS

The ways of the wild are queer
                by human standards
but long ago the Hebraic Old Testament God
                      gave warning when he said,
my ways are not your ways,
                implying
the storm that rages
           out of human understanding,
implying time beyond time,
                 space beyond space,
                 stars beyond stars.
                 I create evil, he said
                 and make the good, that too,
                        in proportion.

Here on my window ledge
                two cardinals,
                male and female,
having lived alone all winter
           in that silence of the solitary
                who seek their own food
                and depend on no one,
suddenly exchange seeds
              in an ancient ritual
              welcoming spring.
They are not too intimate,
             the horn of the beak preventing.
             They are very wild
but grave and dignified—
              at this moment
so much so that if I could
              with the proper manners
I should like to give
             a seed to you.

THE STRAWBERRY BOXES

In the summers the girl workers in the far towns where they
                        packed strawberries
              would occasionally
              write their names on a box
              my name
              is Mary
              my name is
              my name is
              write to me . . .
              they were lonely
              in that place.

I knew from the boxes in our little corner grocery that the girls
                              lived mostly in Arkansas.
When I worked in the hatchery the eggs came in from all over.
                              Sometimes
                              an egg
                              would be penciled
                              write
                              please write
                              my name is Helen
                              my name
                              my name is
                              write
                              I am young.
Working girls from all over America were scribbling names
                              secretively on boxes
                              and hoping
                              somewhere
                              there was
                              the right boy
                              who would
                              answer.
I never wrote because I, too, was a worker, there wasn't time
                              where we turned the eggs
                              in the hundred-degree
                              temperatures
                              in incubators
                              the size of rooms,
                              even then mechanized.
Now, in age, I hope they made out somehow
                              with the local product
                              but I know
                              better.
No man is a hero in his home town. The girls always want someone
                              someone
                              who lives
                              over the

next hill
or in the far
city
one never sees.
Boys and girls I guess we were all lonely and didn't know
what to do,
so the girls
wrote it on eggs
or strawberry boxes:
you there
over the horizon
love me
I am lonely
write.
But then they married and kept on thinking of the strawberry boxes
and the letters
that
never came
and would never
and maybe
the man
left them—
or they
never found one—
luckless.
Maybe it is all solved now in the big cities where everyone
goes,
where no one says
lonely,
no one says
write me.
I think about it sometimes and wonder whether Mary made out
or was it Helen?
they would be
grey now,
their kids

would be
grown up,
but do the girls,
I want to know,
do the children
still write
on the boxes
in the factories:
I am lonely
my name is
my name is.
Life being
as life is
maybe they do.
If I had
strawberry boxes
to pack
I would write
remember me
my name is
a thousand times,
and watch
the trains
haul them away
over the horizon,
but the boxes
are now
green plastic;
I must find
some other way.

CONFRONTATION

And how do you expect to achieve anything
                    without a mob,
triumphed the arrogant young
                    placard carrier
                                fresh from imagined barricades
thus taunting
            a solitary speaker who wanted
                    just solitude,
                    who had heard
angry voices
            since he was born,
                        voices
            between wars and in wars,
            all confident that Utopias
are won with four-letter words
                    and the more hatred
                                the better
                the Utopia
                bound to follow.

When I left him,
                the angry student,
I had no followers
                but the wind that fills
                abandoned cities with dust,
                                I had
no followers
                but the night frost
                that splits stones in
                Saharas of
                        utter silence,
no followers
            in the world

but a stray cat in the dark who
cried from hunger and helplessness
and came
> to me, the stranger,
out of a bush, and then
rolling doubtfully over
> upon his back
he suddenly by choice
> placed
his life in my hands.
He is my follower
> and the night wind
> continues to follow us.
> We avoid

as we can
> the demonstrators
but let it be said
> we are the spokesmen
> for the shadow and the silence,
> the appalling silence
that follows
> and has followed
> and will follow
after the deeds and the invective of the living.
We need no followers,
> ours is the night.

THE HORSE IN COLLEGE HALL

There used to be a small stable once
                in the vault beneath the south tower
                            of College Hall.
An old horse lived there who was led up
                on certain days
        along a curved brick runway
                  to drag
              an antique lawnmower
              over the grass
                    of the Quadrangle.
He enjoyed the sun
                I suppose
and the bright spring

              smell of things,
              and managed a few
              mouthfuls of green
              before they led him
below ground
            till he was needed again.

In that dungeon
           for such it was
              he spent most of his days
              uncomplaining
              perhaps lonely.
I ought to know.
              I was a scholar in that time,
I occupied a cell
              diagonally above him.
It may be we both
              had our thoughts.
              It may be we were both
              lonely for years on end.

Finally they bricked up his passage
                and a machine which ran itself
                        and sputtered
took his familiar place.
                It was less cruel no doubt
                            and no one told me
                what happened to him,
                        his pauses and head tossings
                        and his little banquets
                            of green grass.
Now in the library
                I can see the machines;
                        they tick and buzz
                        computing very rapidly
                        and ejecting on order
bibliographies it took me
                months to compile.

Like the horse I will presently
                be led away.
I can see it in the eyes of those who know best
                            about such things.
It will result in less waste;
                it will be
                        as in the case of the horse
                        less cruel
since there will be merely metal and lights
                which are never lonely
                            and in the end
there will be nothing living
                    to smell the spring grass.
                    Nothing, you understand,
                        we will
                            have replaced ourselves.
I confess I am a little old,
                possibly confused,

but I think it is our object
　　　　　not to be cruel,
　　　　　and to achieve this
many things have first to be done.
　　　　　Among them
　　　　　　　　　old horses
and scholars
　　　　　and then perhaps others
　　　　　and again others
　　　　　　　down to and including
　　　　　　　　　the young
will have to be
　　　　　led away.

I am sorry I never enquired
　　　　　the fate of that old horse
　　　　　　　　　or even
where they hung his harness
　　　　　　　　　for the last time.
Perhaps even then I was actually
　　　　　　　　a little afraid to ask.
I should not say this.
　　　　　　　It is definitely our object
　　　　　　　　　not to be cruel.
They smoothed out the grass and filled in the earth
　　　　　　　　I remember
　　　　　　　　　over his little walkway.
Only I can remember
　　　　　　　where it was.
No one, I suspect, will do this for man,
　　　　　　　certainly not the machines.
Our kindness will have been to ourselves.
　　　　　　　I think now
　　　　what is often called
　　　　　　　total.

THINK THAT I SPOKE TO YOU

Poetry is the art of the ephemeral
                                    someone has said,
                                                        and another,
the art of the continually renewed or always present.
                                    Obviously
the one was probably
                        looking at a butterfly, the other
at a boulder or
                the fall of a wave. I
love all these things
                    but I know
boulders are eaten by tiny lichens
                                    distilling acid
and the one wave
                    is not the next wave
any more than the butterfly,
                                though I hope, barring insecticides,
that the migratory Monarchs may flutter
                                            through a thousand springs.

                                        No,
we are the ephemerals,
                        even the crowd that passes
and is
        constantly renewed.
                            Oh we are the ephemerals
because we think
                    and the thoughts are not ever
voiced by the same tongues
                            in the same way.
Think of me
                standing far away
                in a wild-rose thicket

or by those huge glacial erratics
whose strength I so much
needed,
but could not absorb.
Think that I spoke to you
and was not heard and the thought
was presently gone,
not even a poem formulated,
not even
an articulate cry,
a distressed sound rather,
lost on a wind that
if it circled the world
would not repeat
what it heard.
Think of me then
with my hand
half raised
trying to say
and someone else,
by fortune, or no one
trying to hear.
That is a poem.

THE ROPE

I used to carry a frayed rope in my hand
upon the speaker's rostrum,
                      try to tell
my students this:
                  that there was a similar rope
as loosely frayed
                  that bound them to the past,
a rope that somewhere ran
            to an old salt-oozing eye
in the deep sea,
               and that strange eye
still stared from underneath their brows
                          full at me,
just as the interlocked vertebrae of their dextrous spines
                      was long ago
a fish's gift,
             just as
their lungs had labored gasping in a swamp
to serve a fish's needs,
               and these frayed strands
of the rope I held
            ran back and back
                          to individual and diverse times
in sea and swamp and forest,
                 twisted finally
into our living substance, hidden in ourselves
that code of DNA,
           that secret spiral ladder
made up of bits and pieces of
               the past that never dies
but lives entwined in us,
        our spines uptilted in a forest attic;
        our foot, so tendon-bound

and twisted over,
                    a re-engineered bent
                                    climbing pad
renewed to walk on grass;
                    our fingers quick
                            with stones;
our brains
                dreaming lost ancient dreams
as well as throwing
                    ropes in the air as though to catch
what is uncatchable—
                            the future.
We can ask only the question
                    nor can we be
                            answered save through signs.

By many primitive fires around the world
                            man has
employed the rope trick of the Indian fakirs,
                            striven to climb
out of himself to heaven,
                    forever scaled
the giant beanstalk of himself,
                        been cast
forever down,
                    arose and climbed again.
Here holding
            before a scientific audience
a plain, unmagical ordinary rope of hemp
                    I suddenly find
that, having made ascent, by weeping eye, salt-crusted fin,
                            and wrigglings learned
piercing the downpour of a continent
                    to reach this trembling platform,
it is my intent
            to stay and cast

                              the wondrous rope still farther.
Fakir, mystic I may be, but this,
this is the way we came, the way
                              of the invisible rope
in the beginning cast
                              somewhere in the Devonian darkness
                                        or below.
This is what instructed seers enact,
                    unknowing the precise sense
in which they cast but casting rope or thread
                              always above them
by dimly smoking fires
                    or using
an old, old symbolism
                    and climbing
                              before an audience
the ever-growing tree
                    up which there run
                              animals in pursuit.

This is a heavy time to cast my rope.
I stand unmagical
                    knowing only
the trick was done far back and must be done again.

I let the cord fall and I climb on words,
          swaying, ascending,
          desperate, as man
in the black dark has always swung and climbed
          toward some far sky lord he has never seen,
assembling along the ever-lengthening rope
his own dismantled self, the eye that weeps
                              salt tears
reborn,
          the mind
cleansed of its treason and foul unbelief.

Believe, oh do believe;
        look up,
                the rope is there
lent by that devious double agent, night.
        Oh now we know
the rope is hidden in ourselves to climb.

OTHER DIMENSIONS

In a hall of mirrors one sees oneself endlessly repeated
       but the images are equal,
          they are the same face
            in a moment of time.
The alternative days of a life stretch almost
                     to infinity and are different
                        in years
                        and episodes.
Why one is real
         and the others remain
        mere unexploited potential
         no one knows
           but sometimes
I can feel them stirring
         and remember
          where the road diverged,
        but not
          why one path was chosen
          and not the other.

Be honest, no one knows except the unseen player. I remember
          the poor years
          when
          drifting into
          any eddy
          I might have
          remained there—
night watchman, hatchery worker, honest things,
I think I did them well enough, but the times
          were
          changing.
          One thinks
          of darker episodes

in the streets of night
and of youth.
That time they talked of running liquor and the price
paid to Capone's
truck drivers,
I listened but
it was a long way
to Chicago
and the connections
didn't carry
that far.
It was the time
of the big money for some
on the other side
of the tracks
and I was one.
It was, I believe now, just the difference between
the country mouse
and the city rat.
I knew too little for
abstract morality;
I might just as well
have been gunned down
in an alley.
That is one dead face in the mirror, one genuine potentiality
not very like
the scholar among his books.

There was also the big sea-going engineer with whom
I struck an acquaintance
and swapped stories
on a train when I
was a graduate student.
Think of it as a near thing, for I
was a reader of Conrad and the man
offered to get me through

a picket line to help him take
a short-handed freighter
out to sea.
What kind of face would I be wearing now, I wonder,
or would it be
down there with the fishes
under the Murmansk run?
And the wildcat oil driller swapping whiskies
on some remote train in Wyoming
before my life was settled,
speaking
wistfully of his daughter
and trying
to lure me as his
geologist
when I was already
promised
to another job.
I liked them all, except that the unseen player
willed it otherwise.
I had already given my word
to be elsewhere
when they approached me.
It was no more than that—
too late, too late
for other lives,
the ones
I really wanted.
I was ignorant, friendly, capable of flowing
into any guise
save that some dubious compass
kept swinging me
to another time
and would give me
after a while

the face I carry
and no rest.
Once, long ago, I clung to the tender of a midnight limited
hurtling down the long plains
from the Rockies.
Hundreds of miles later I remember as in a dream
crying to a companion
above the battering
of the wheels,
arousing from exhaustion
on the rocking
iron ladder
to realize
I was talking
to phantoms,
that I was
just preparing
against the frantic messages
of my numbed body
to slide downward
into sleep.
We slowed for a station and I swung off,
fully conscious by then
and terrified
but still—
how would it be to nod and slip down into
the roaring dark
in youth
hearing far off
the train whistle
fading
far off,
fading
into another time
beyond you

leaving you forever
to the silence
and the peace?
It happened to many in those years of the great wandering.
Sometimes now, sleeping very little, I think of train roofs
I have slept soundly on
and the night
on that swaying ladder
above the wheels.
The life that almost ended
draws me with a strange attraction. I can feel it stirring.
It almost lives,
perhaps because it was in me
realized,
perhaps also
because
it has something to do
with sleep.

AN OWL'S DAY

Crouched in a rock shelter on this high escarpment
I watch rain curtain the valley, concealing it
like another century, but up here under the overhang
all is dry dust. A bone needle and a flint knife
              turned up by pack rats
lie on the surface with a few owl pellets that, minutely dissected,
reveal the white bones of rodents and a twist of fur
spat out as an afterthought, just as the bits and rejects
of the mind must more invisibly
return to earth.
          It is strange to find
the bones of the great bird himself in a similar tangle,
the luminous eyes that always
            spelled wisdom in lost cultures,
the ear that heard
            every whisper on the night wind,
all sunk into fragments thin as the eggshell
from which they arose.

Down there beneath the rain cloud
              is another century
not surely mine.
          I sit up here in the dust
          among the pellets and bones
trying the haft of the flint knife in my hand
              trying
to sort what is dust in my mind
            from what is dust
in this abandoned shelter.
           My effort is not very successful,
not after the birds' wisdom has failed,
          not after
          rain has blinded my vision,

not after
            all our days are dried pellets of bone,
but listen, I
am not new here.

I have seen an owl follow a hawk's flight
                  so far
I took what he saw on faith because of his eyes;
               now all darkens, yes, but
I am not new here.
            The century in the green valley does not matter.
I have my own way of staring into the sun.
The stone knife is not new.
            I am a man, with a man's sight for such things,
A million centuries can go or come here,
I will see them momentarily, reading beyond past and future,
        not caring in which century lies the rain cloud
          or if I drop
          descending the rock slide
a flint knife
         or a cartridge case.
I am a man with my own way of seeing
          just as the owl saw
          but he in his way
as I in mine.
       Even though we darken
       even though we sleep
       we have ranged far
and left these little pellets for the wind to gather,
he, the far bits of an owl's day,
I, something more nebulous seen across a storm cloud,
better not to be left here
lest the pack rats carry it out of its context
like this stone knife in the dust.

OREGON TRAIL

It is spring somewhere beyond

                Chimney Rock

                on the old

                Oregon trail now.

I remember the time

                when the ruts of the wagons

                      could still be seen across

                                    a half mile

                of unbroken short-grass prairie

as though

                in that high air

                they had just passed,

the rolling Conestoga wagons
                              heavy-freighted
                                   for the Sierras,
                                   as though time was
only yesterday,
                         as though, if one hurried,
a fast horse
                    with good wind
                    would bring you
                              to the buckskinned outriders
                              and the lined brown women
                              with sunbonnets,
the grandmothers,
                         the fathers,
                         children who became
                         the forest cutters,
                         wheat raisers,
                                        gold seekers,
                                        sharpshooters,
                         range killers,
                              users of
                              the first Colts in
                              the cattle wars
                              or at the gamblers' tables—
a time a fast horse
                    might still catch up with
almost anything.

I whirl my animal
three times about
and bend over the tracks
trampling uncertainly.
                    It is time to go home.
But the other time is there
                         tempting
                         just beyond the horizon.

[118]

I back off reluctantly
            and out of some shamed courtesy
            slip my spectacles
            into my pocket
                and raise my hand
                saying a wordless
                          goodbye.

Index of Titles and First Lines

INDEX OF TITLES AND FIRST LINES

About the Author

Loren Eiseley was born and spent his boyhood among the salt flats and sunflower forests of eastern Nebraska and on the high plains beyond the 99th meridian. Child of the marriage of a prairie artist and a one-time itinerant actor, Dr. Eiseley, in spite of the handicaps of poverty, was early exposed to the magic of poetry through the beautiful trained voice of his father and through his mother to an intense appreciation for the beauties of the natural world. The vicissitudes of the great depression led him successively from aimless drifter, to fossil hunter, to sporadic college student, and finally to a career in science culminating in the holding of a distinguished chair in anthropology at the University of Pennsylvania. Loren Eiseley's prose, long noted for its poetic quality, has won him among other honors the distinction of being an elected member of the National Institute of Arts and Letters.